Cosmo's
Naughty
Notes

Surprise your guy with them!

100 Sexy Stickies
To Tease, Tantalize, and Turn On Your Man

From the Editors of COSMOPOLITAN

D0987869

Welcome to *Cosmo*'s Naughty Notes!

This little book is jam-packed with 100 sexy stickies specially designed to delight, surprise, and seduce any man. Whether you use them to pay him a carnal compliment, reveal a taboo fantasy, or suggest a randy rendezvous, these notes are a surefire way to ignite his passion. You can also make your next special occasion sizzle with red-hot wishes for his birthday, Valentine's Day, the Fourth of July, and more. Plus, you'll find blank stickies in the back so that you can write your very own naughty notes—for his eyes only, of course. All you do is peel off a note and leave it on his pillow, dashboard, bathroom mirror, or wherever he might find it....Then watch his temperature rise!

—The Editors of *Cosmopolitan*

I won't bite...
unless you beg for it.

_____'s

TO DO LIST:

- ☑ **Brazilian wax**
- ☑ **Stretch**
- ☐ _____

Know what
I could use
right now?

Your lips
on mine.

XOXOXO

Cheer up, handsome.

I see oral sex in your future.

Did I ever
tell you
I was voted
most flexible
in my
yoga class?

CARNAL COUPON

Entitles

_____

to one
lay-there-and-love-it
sack session

CARNAL COUPON

CARNAL COUPON

PLEASE
LEAVE YOUR
CLOTHES
AT THE
DOOR.

I'm in need
of some
stress relief.

Got any ideas?

XOXOXO

I DARE YOU...

...TO LEAVE THE LIGHTS ON. I WANT TO SEE EVERYTHING.

Since we're going to visit my family, I have to warn you: The sight of my twin bed makes me want to do things that would shock my parents.

Some guys turn heads.
You inspire 360-degree gawking.

Take your pick:

- [ ] Long kiss
- [ ] Deep kiss
- [ ] Wet kiss
- [ ] All of the above

Thanks for
last night...

and tonight.

See you later.

XOXOXO

I'd bend over backward for you. Can I prove it later tonight?

Please
hand over
your jeans.
I'll return them
to you in an
hour...or however
long it takes
to blow
your mind.

Instead of getting you a cheesy Valentine's gift, I thought I'd just ravage your body instead.

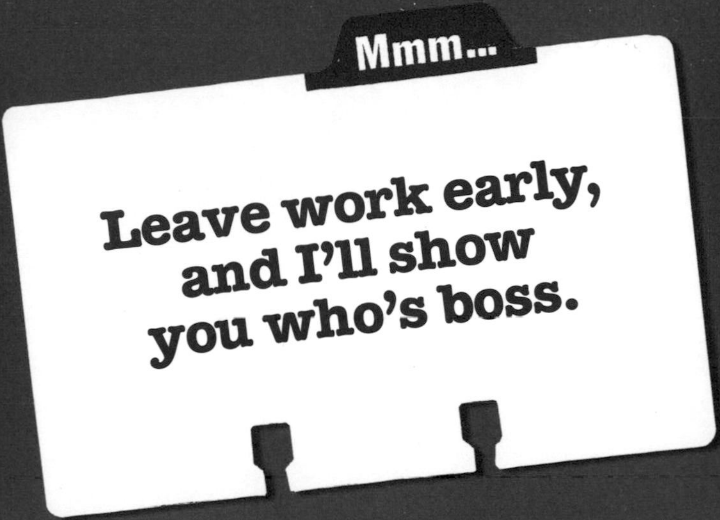
Mmm...
Leave work early, and I'll show you who's boss.

ALL *my* GIRL friends *think* you're HOT.

It's cold and
raining outside.
Let's stay
in bed all day
and keep each
other warm.

XOXOXO

I woke up in
a giving mood.
Be sure to
hurry home
tonight.

I'm rereading all the classics.

THE COSMO
KAMA SUTRA
77 mind-blowing
sex positions

The Editors of COSMOPOLITAN

Tonight I plan to tackle *The Cosmo Kama Sutra.*

A FEW OF

_____'S

FAVORITE THINGS:

- ☑ **Your face**
- ☑ **Your lips**
- ☑ **Your eyes**
- ☑ **Your** _____

The Guinness
Book called.
They said
your stamina
is record
breaking.

To: _____

For your birthday,
I've decided to
grant you that one
frisky wish you've
been begging for.

Love: _____

Call your
roommate and
tell him
you won't be
coming home
tonight.

XOXOXO

Grab the
check and
skip dessert,
because I have
something better
waiting for
you at home.

I'm dying
to take
another trip
south of
your border.

Let's make this a red-hot holiday season!

This bad girl deserves a spanking.

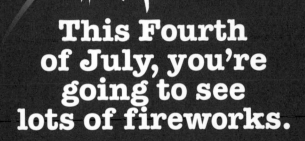

This Fourth
of July, you're
going to see
lots of fireworks.

Then we'll
go see the
ones outside.

Let's do a blind taste test:

I'll hide a dab
of honey
on my body
and you
have to use
your tongue
to find it.

CARNAL COUPON

Entitles

to one mind-blowing oral sex session

CARNAL COUPON

CARNAL COUPON

Stressed?
I know just the
massage oil
that will rub
that out.

You know
that girl who
dumped you?
I'm thinking of
writing her a
thank-you note.

XOXOXO

All I CAN say is WOW.

this vacation
so hot,

we won't be
able to show
anyone
our photos.

I'm so wound up.
Would you mind
meeting me
in the bedroom
to work out
some kinks?

One New Year's resolution I need you to help me keep: taking our sex life to the next level.

It's laundry night....Know what that means? I'm not wearing any undies.

XOXOXO

If you like
how I look
with my
clothes on,
just wait
until you
see me naked.

Come here, I'll kiss it and make it better. Everywhere.

Oh Yeah!

Congrats on your promotion!

Now it's my turn to give you a raise!

My alarm clock
is on the fritz.
Can you
think of an
effective way
to rouse me?

Bring the whipped cream.

Dessert is on me tonight.

I'm thinking about you right now. Hope I'm not near any mind readers.

XOXOXO

...TO WAKE
UP THE
NEIGHBORS.

Why talk when there are so many other fun ways to use our mouths?

I'M ON A HIGH
C.A.R.B. DIET:

CRAVING

A

RIPPED

BOD

INDULGE ME?

Right now,
as you're
reading this,
I'm thinking
about being
in bed with you.

XOXOXO

Want a
quick break
from watching
the game?
I'll give you a
halftime show
you'll never
forget.

Pretend it's your birthday tonight,

because I have a gift you won't be able to wait another day for.

Think the
sex is good
now? Well,
guess what...
it only gets
better.

NO SHIRT.
NO SHOES.
FULL SERVICE!

Meet me in the car in five minutes. I'll be in the backseat, waiting for a...ride.

XOXOXO

You may want to soundproof your walls...

'cause I make a lot of noise.

memo

TO: _____

FROM: _____

Studies show that the more below-the-belt pleasure I give you, the better you'll perform at work.

Let's test it out.

JUST *read* this **month's** COSMO.

We **HAVE** HOMEWORK!

Mark this date down:

Calendar

It's the first time we're going to

_____

(fill in sex act here)

Don't do
much at the
gym....

Save energy
for later.

XOXOXO

It's your call:
black lace
thong
or nothing
at all?

I know you're in a bad mood.

Let me take off your boxers, and I promise you'll feel 10 times better.

CARNAL COUPON

Entitles

to one lusty lap dance

CARNAL COUPON

CARNAL COUPON

They say
absence makes
the heart
grow fonder.
Does it
make other
things grow
too?

I found
my old
cheerleading
uniform.

It still fits.

GIVE ME AN
OOOOH!

You know what I'm thankful for this year? Having your body as my own personal playground.

XOXOXO

Fantasies
are nice.

Reality
is better.

Free tonight?

Just one more
reason to
get over that cold:
a night of wild,
wake-the-neighbors
sex with me.

I'd like to borrow your mouth for the entire day.
Hope you can handle it.

I think you
need a
new position
at work:

OFFICE USE ONLY!

doggie-style,
with me over
your desk.

I've yet to
meet a man
who can keep
up with me.
No pressure.

You spoil me rotten.

I like that in a man.

...TO MAKE
MY TOES CURL...

TWICE IN
A ROW.

YOU
+
ME
-
CLOTHES
=
A LOT
OF FUN!

Fill in the blanks:

"I love it when you start touching me _____,

then move down to my _____,

then finish off by licking my _____."

I don't
know how to
thank you,
so I'll stick with
the standby:
sex so good
you won't
know what
hit you.

I feel kind of
sorry for all
those other guys
out there.
You're just so
much hotter.

XOXOXO

memo

TO: _____

FROM: _____

Tell your boss that
you have to leave
early today, then meet
me at my place.

Be my sex slave for the next hour.

You must fulfill every risqué request.

If you
were any
yummier,
I'd have
to go on
a diet.

Let's leave the windows open tonight. No one in our neighborhood will want to miss this show.

Some girls are
too sweet to
speak up in bed.

I'm not one
of them.

xoxoxo

Let's play
doctor.

IT'S official. 69 is my favorite number.

Ever thought of installing a mirror on your bedroom ceiling? Maybe you should.

Forget the mile-high
club. Next time
we board a
plane, you're
mine before we
leave the gate.

_____

_____

_____

_____

_____

_____

memo

TO: _____

FROM: _____

_____

_____

_____

_____

_____

_____

10 9 8 7 6 5 4 3 2 1

COSMOPOLITAN

Edited by John Searles
Book Design by Peter Perron
Written by Michele Promaulayko, Riann Smith,
Jennifer Benjamin, Meaghan Buchan
Additional Text by Christie Griffin

Editor-in-Chief Kate White
Design Director Ann P. Kwong

Cosmopolitan and Hearst Books are trademarks of Hearst Communications, Inc.

cosmopolitan.com

For information about custom editions, special sales, premium and corporate purchases, please contact Sterling Special Sales Department at 800-805-5489 or specialsales@sterlingpub.com.

Distributed in Canada by Sterling Publishing
c/o Canadian Manda Group, 165 Dufferin Street
Toronto, Ontario, Canada M6K 3H6

Distributed in Australia by Capricorn Link (Australia) Pty. Ltd.
P.O. Box 704, Windsor, NSW 2756 Australia

Manufactured in China

ISBN-13: 978-1-58816-599-2
ISBN-10: 1-58816-599-X